Open Secrets

A Play

Katy Darby

SAMUELFRENCH-LONDON.CO.UK
SAMUELFRENCH.COM

OPEN SECRETS

First produced at the Tristran Bates Theatre, 1a Tower Street, London WC2, on 14th-17th October 2003, with the following cast of characters:

Tobias	Ray Newe
Casey	Hannah Lean
Leila	Zoe Gardner

Directed by Laura Baggaley
Designed by Laura Baggaley
Lighting by Luke Girling

CHARACTERS

Tobias, 30, a chef, any ethnicity, male Cockney, nearly through a doctorate in moral philosophy, working to meet rising tuition fees. He reads while he cooks, when he does cook. He's eking out his days in a sinecure until he can become a full time academic.

Casey, early to mid 20s, a waitress, any ethnicity, and T-shirt entrepreneur *manqué*; all she needs is a bit of capital to realize her dreams. She and Tobias are going out.

Leila, mid 20s to early 30s, any ethnicity. A spy who has been working for MI6 since graduation. She has just been simultaneously dumped and fired by her boyfriend.

The action takes place in a tapas bar and kitchen

Time — the present

OPEN SECRETS

A tapas bar and kitchen. Monday, 7 p.m.

The stage is split into two rooms and is effectively a cross-section through a tapas bar L and kitchen R. There is a communicating door or doorway, possibly with one of those plastic strip curtains, between bar and kitchen. The bar has a counter, a couple of bar stools and perhaps a table for effect in the corner. Above the bar is a blackboard with the day's specials on it. The kitchen should be as realistic as possible, although it could consist merely of a fridge and a microwave. There are kitchen units and worktops and a kitchen chair. The kitchen is spotless, with a pile of microwaveable meals, a bag of tortillas and a jar of cheese sauce or salsa placed neatly on one surface, ready for the night's food orders

The Lights come up on Casey wiping down the kitchen surfaces listlessly as Tobias sits straddling a kitchen chair Christine Keeler style, reading a library book on Wittgenstein. A "Hits of the 80s" compilation plays in the background. It is about 7 p.m. on a Monday night — the dead zone

Tobias I'll do that. Sit down and relax.
Casey You're reading.
Tobias It's not very interesting.
Casey (*a rhetorical question*) When's your thesis due?
Tobias Two weeks time.
Casey Exactly. I'll do this. (*She continues to clean*)
Tobias (*putting down his book*) Come here.
Casey (*coming over*) What?

He pulls her down by her tie to kiss her

Tobias Thanks.

Casey All part of the job, sir.

Tobias Well, not strictly speaking, no. Part of my job. But I'll let you keep my tips.

Casey Best not. I'd only abscond to Rio.

Tobias Seriously, I'm really grateful. Most people would have to pay somebody to do this for them, whereas I have my own domestic slave chained to the kitchen sink.

Casey picks up one of the frozen food packets and contemplates it

Casey Ever been beaten to death with frozen lasagne?

Tobias Sounds kinky.

Casey puts down the packet

Casey This time I'll let you live, but only because Helen would deduct the wasted food from my wages.

Tobias Cheers, Casey. (*He puts down his book*) Listen, I'll make us something nice for tonight. Not this junk-food crap, something with green stuff in it. And as soon as I get my thesis finished I promise to become a functioning human being again, too. How does that sound?

Casey Optimistic. (*Pause*) What are you reading?

Tobias The *Little Book of Wittgenstein*.

Casey Any relation to the *Tiny Book of Hugs*?

Tobias I'm glad you asked. They're very similar in many ways, except that *Tractatus Logico-Philosophicus* is slightly larger and has fewer hugs.

Casey Shame.

Pause. She wipes desultorily, looking at her watch. She is bored and wants Tobias to talk to her

Has it got any quotable quotes in it?

Tobias closes the book and smiles. He knows what this is about

Tobias Is this for your T-shirt enterprise?

Casey Maybe.

Tobias Well, there's a couple in here, but I'm not sure whether Uncle Ludwig's out of copyright yet. All the little Wittgensteins might come down on you like a ton of bricks.

Casey I'll take that risk.

Tobias All right. (*He flips through the pages to one with a bent corner*) How about: "Someone who knows too much finds it hard not to lie".

Casey Oh yes, I *like* that. Don't know if the paying public would want it emblazoned across their chests, mind you. We need something with a little more dash and panache.

Tobias What have you got so far?

Casey A couple of phrases, a couple of copyright infringements on eighties cartoons: not enough to build a million-pound business out of, really.

Tobias Eat your heart out, Anita Roddick.

Casey Oi! It's a lot more practical as a life-plan than being a chef with a Doctorate in Philosophy.

Tobias Being a waitress with a potential T-shirt empire?

Casey And an MBA. Anyway, this is my year off. If it doesn't work out I'll go to KPMG or somewhere.

Tobias For a business graduate you're very reluctant to actually work in business.

Casey I *do* want to work in business — *my* business. I just don't want to work my arse off for shareholder profits and the undeserved benefit of my fat-cat boss. I want to succeed on my own terms in my own marketplace.

Tobias Hence waitressing, of course.

Casey At least I get a little human interaction, Professor Sartre.

Tobias The lack of human interaction is exactly what I love about this job. People leave chefs alone: they have a reputation for being violent and unpredictable.

Casey Is that a hint for me to sod off?

Tobias No! Well … I do have to finish this chapter.

Casey Point taken. The surfaces in the bar are fogging over a bit anyway. Better crack out the duster, eh?

She leaves the kitchen, going through into the empty bar area and fooling around with the cocktail sticks, etc. There is really nothing to do, so she swipes a paper from under the bar and sits on a stool at the counter, reading it. Idly she picks a couple of olives from the courtesy bowl in front of her and chomps them. Meanwhile, next door, Tobias is becoming increasingly bored with his book, and fitful. Eventually he gives up reading it, instead balancing it carefully, face down and open, on his head. (NB: this is easier with a hardback) He remains in this position, staring blankly out at the audience

Tobias I think, therefore I am — a chef.
Casey You talking to yourself?
Tobias Yes, but I never listen to a word I say.
Casey Very wise of you.

Pause

Tobias What are your slogans?
Casey For my T-shirts?
Tobias Of course.
Casey Top secret.
Tobias That's one of them?
Casey No, I mean they're highly confidential.
Tobias Ah go on, tell me. I promise not to go to the papers.

Casey suddenly grins enormously and shuts her paper. She gets down off the bar stool and goes around to the back of the bar, from under which she extracts a plastic bag with a couple of T-shirts in it. She pokes her head around the doorway to the kitchen

Casey I can do better than that. I can show you. (*She holds up the bag*)
Tobias You got them done? Great! How much?
Casey Too much, but I needed some samples and I'm thinking of offsetting the cost against my birthday.

Tobias You mean I'm paying?
Casey Sweet of you to offer! This is the first one.

She whips her tie off — it's on elastic — and takes off her white shirt. She should probably be wearing a bra, but it's not obligatory. She pulls a white T-shirt, from the bag, over her head: in a black handwriting font across the chest it reads: "Hang Louche"

Tobias Hang louche! Nice! Did you come up with that yourself?
  Casey (*insulted*) Yes, actually.
Tobias Just wondering. If it's any help, I'd buy that T-shirt immediately even if I wasn't already obliged to.
Casey Thank you, darling. (*She kisses him lightly*) Next one.

She changes again. The next one reads in a gold or blue wacky font on a pink shirt (or in black on white) "Kitsch Me Quick". Tobias bursts out laughing

Tobias Oh, that's superb. I'd swap my granny for that one. No wonder you didn't want Uncle Ludwig on the front.
Casey Told you I was a slogan genius. All I need is a measly couple of grand and then I could take over the world with my casualwear.

Tobias looks at his watch

Tobias Listen, Casey, you'd better watch it. Helen mentioned that she might be coming in this evening. She didn't say when but you know what she's like.
Casey Oh Christ, not another spot-inspection. She's not in the army any more, doesn't she realize that? This isn't café bloody boot camp.
Tobias Don't tell her that, the shock might prove too much.
Casey Damn, I'd better get changed. At least the place is spotless. (*She pulls her shirt and tie back on*) Surfaces you could eat your dinner off, no thanks to you.
Tobias To paraphrase Wittgenstein, "Someone who reads too much finds it hard not to laze".

Casey You can make me some guacamole if you're feeling underworked.
Tobias God, I'm not *that* bored.

There is a sound of a door opening and closing

Leila walks into the bar with an expensive and secure-looking briefcase, preferably silver. She is wearing a conservative business suit and shirt, full make-up, high heels and an expression of extreme ire. She glances around, then heads for the bar

Casey Hell, it's her already! Wish me luck.
Tobias Show me your insincere smile.

Casey displays a horrible rictus

You'll do.

Tobias gets up, shoves the chair out of sight and hides the book. Casey comes out to the bar. During the following, Tobias empties out the tortilla chips and dumps salsa on them and then starts reading his book surreptitioustly

Casey Sorry, Helen, I was just — (*She clocks that Leila is a customer*) Oh, sorry I thought you were — what can I get you?
Leila Have you got any offers on drinks?
Casey Well, we have to do something to entice people in here on a Monday, so it's Happy Hour on Sol all night.

Leila makes a face

Or we've got a jug of any house cocktail for a tenner.
Leila How big are the jugs?
Casey Two pints.
Leila Sounds perfect.

Leila sits down on a bar stool, dumping the briefcase under the bar stool next to her, and begins to pick at the olives. Casey raises her eyebrows

Casey OK — which one would you like?
Leila Any. What have you got?
Casey Well, there's the Screwdriver, Daiquiris, White Russian,
  Long Island Iced Tea, Margarita ——
Leila What's the one with Coke in it?
Casey Long Island.
Leila That one.

*Casey begins to make a jug of it — several shots of five white spirits,
lemon juice and Coke from a bottle*

Casey (*finally*) Hard day, eh?
Leila (*almost puzzled, it has been the worst day of her life*) Um
  …yeah.
Casey How many glasses?
Leila Just a straw, thanks.

Casey is not sure if she's joking. She hesitates

  Sorry, I'm being facetious. One glass. Nobody will be joining me
  but I hope your other customers won't mind if I stay here and get
  quietly drunk in the corner.
Casey I'm sure they won't object. Would you like to run a tab?
Leila Yeah, why not? It's on expenses. (*She hands over her card*)
Casey Thanks, Ms — Ramone.
Leila Don't thank me, thank the Government.
Casey I wish they'd buy me a drink occasionally.
Leila No you don't.
Casey Excuse me just for a moment.

*Casey goes into the kitchen. Tobias, who is reading his book
surreptitiously, starts violently*

Tobias Bloody hell, don't do that. I thought you were Helen. How
  is she? Got her stomping boots on?
Casey No, no, the coast is clear. It wasn't her, it's just a customer.

Tobias A customer? Blimey, where's the emergency handbook? What are we supposed to do with one of those?

Casey I think if I just feed her alcohol until she falls over she'll be immensely grateful.

Tobias Oh dear, one of those. Is she a talker?

Casey Don't know yet. Think she might be.

Tobias Let me know if you need any help out there.

Casey I'll yell if she expresses an interest in Wittgenstein.

Tobias Stranger things have happened.

He settles back into his chair and continues reading as Casey goes back out to the bar area, where Leila is drinking her cocktail and humming or singing along to one of the 80s' hits

Leila I love this one. I remember dancing to it when I was about fifteen.

Casey Happy days?

Leila Happier. Mind you, the day my dog got ran over when I was eight is comparing pretty favourably at the moment.

Casey Harsh.

Leila Yeah, harsh.

Pause

Casey Man trouble or job trouble?

Leila Try both.

Casey (*joking*) Not sleeping with your boss, are you?

Leila (*bitterly*) Not since he fired me, no.

Casey Ooh. Oh. Ah.

A pause. Casey wipes glasses, Leila drinks steadily

So, what did you, ah, do?

Leila Nothing! He just — oh, I see what you mean. Professionally. I can't tell you.

Casey Why not?

Leila Let me put it this way, rather: I could tell you, but I'd have to
   kill you. (*She taps the side of her nose portentously*)
Casey Oh. Right.

*She finishes wiping a couple of glasses and takes them out to the
kitchen, where Tobias is reading again. He looks up*

Tobias Chatty, is she?
Casey Well, sort of. (*With childish excitement*) I think she's a *spy*
Tobias Wow, *cool*! Let's ask to see her *gun*!
Casey No, seriously, she could be. The MI6 building's only up the
   road. And Helen's always going on about how many spies we
   must get in here but we just ——
Tobias — don't know it, yeah, I know. Well, great. Maybe she'll
   recruit us and pay us a massive retainer to eavesdrop on her
   colleagues.
Casey That would be nice, but I think this evening she's mostly
   going to bitch about her boss and share her broken heart.
Tobias I could give her the consolations of philosophy.
Casey I think she might pay you not to.
Tobias Score!
Leila (*calling*) Miss! Um, sorry, I don't know your name.

Casey backs out of the kitchen, waving

Casey Duty calls … Yes, madam?
Leila Could I see your food menu?

*Casey gestures above her head to the blackboard with the day's
specials on it*

Casey It's all up there.
Leila Oh, right … what's the lasagne like?
Casey Honestly?
Leila If you're allowed.
Casey Frozen. And not very nice.

Leila Oh. What's fresh?

Casey Um … the olives?

Leila Listen, never mind, I'll just have some chips and salsa.

Casey Good choice. I'll just tell the chef. (*She goes through to the kitchen*)

Tobias is making notes on a menu pad and sticking them in his book

Got a job for you.

Tobias Hmm?

Casey Our Jane Bond wants — oh, you've done it already. (*She scoops up the bowl of tortilla and salsa and takes it out to Leila*)

Tobias Oi, that was mine! Bloody customers.

Casey (*to Leila*) Here you go.

Leila Thanks. Listen, can I ask you a personal question?

Casey (*warily*) OK …

Leila Have you got a boyfriend?

Casey Well — yeah.

Leila Is he good to you? I mean, romantic, considerate, calls when he says he will, doesn't stay out late … all that.

Casey (*pointedly and loudly, so that Tobias can hear*) He's all right, I suppose. (*Normally*) But we've both got money worries. I just can't see a way out of it, really. I'd do anything, really, anything to get a bit of extra cash — actually, make that a lot of extra cash.

Leila Murder? Scandal? Sell your story to the papers?

Pause. Casey smiles limply

I suppose there's always lap-dancing.

Casey Don't think I haven't thought about it. Tobias would go nuts, though. He'd say I was abetting the patriarchy by participating in my own degradation.

Leila Would he now? Bit of a moral stickler, is he?

Casey (*apologetically*) He's a bit overworked at the moment.

Leila Wish I was. Sorry, I don't mean to bang on … This cocktail is great by the way.

Casey Thanks. One of my few marketable skills.
Leila Would that I had some.
Casey What about your, y'know … *job*?
Leila My expertise isn't what you might call easily transferable.
   Plus I got fired. How does that look?
Casey Hey, there's always waitressing.
Leila Don't even joke. Oops. Sorry, I didn't mean to imply that it
   was ——
Casey Rubbish? That's all right. It is. The quickest way to come to
   hate everybody is to take a job in a service industry. Some people
   are nice, of course, but sometimes I think most of the customers
   here are on day release from Strangeways.
Leila So you must have something you really want to do?
Casey Of course. Every waitress has a dream. It's what helps them
   carry on being waitresses. If there was an epidemic of pessimism
   every restaurant and bar in the country would fold.
Leila What is it? Do you mind if I ask?
Casey No, of course not. I — it sounds really silly now.
Leila Go on. Do you have a cigarette?
Casey Sorry, I don't smoke.
Leila Nor do I. I gave up three years ago but I really want one now,
   for some reason.
Casey I'll ask the chef. He studies philosophy, he's bound to be able
   to roll you one.
Leila Oh yes. Like Sartre.

Casey walks into the kitchen and throws a towel at Tobias

Casey All right, it's your shift. Our lady wants a fag and I've got
   to call Helen and reassure her that the place isn't on fire. Back in
   five. (*She starts to move off* R)
Tobias She's not going to abuse me for being a man, is she?
Casey Don't be scared, she'll love you for giving her tobacco.

Casey exits

*Tobias takes a tobacco tin out of his pocket, sticks his book in his
apron, and goes out to the bar*

Tobias How are the chips? All right?

Leila Fine thanks. It's a bit quiet in here tonight, isn't it?

Tobias (*rolling a cigarette*) Helen usually scares people away. She's our boss. On the few nights she isn't in, the customers think it's a cunning double bluff and avoid this place anyway, just in case.

Leila You know, you really remind me of someone.

Tobias Oh really? Who?

Leila My ex-boyfriend.

Tobias (*winking*) Good looking bloke, is he?

Leila (*blankly*) Not really, no.

Tobias Oh. Must be the sparkling personality, then.

Leila He's a bastard.

Tobias Listen, do you want this cigarette or what?

Leila Oh, of course — I'm sorry, I was just thinking out loud. No offence meant.

Tobias Just please don't give me the "all men are bastards" line.

Leila Do you get that a lot?

Tobias Not generally to my face, but I hear it often enough from women about other men.

Leila And you don't think it might be justified?

Tobias Sometimes. Not always.

Leila Do you have a girlfriend?

Tobias (*defensively*) Yes.

Leila (*taking the cigarette from his hands and lighting it with the matches in the ashtray*) I'm surprised.

Tobias You're welcome.

Leila Forgive me. I've just been fired and dumped by my ex for sleeping with him.

Tobias Seems a bit excessive.

Leila He accused me of not being able to keep my mind on the job.

Tobias Which one?

Leila Ha ha. My work. That's not the real reason, though. He wants to get rid of me because *he*'s angling for promotion and *he* can't afford a scandal. Some people were starting to suspect — his wife was one of them, in fact, so he got rid of *me*. No pension, no golden handshake, no references at all. Bugger all.

Tobias Tough break.

Leila (*girly, winsome*) All I want is a little revenge.

Tobias Well, can't you sue him for unfair dismissal or something?

Leila (*putting a finger to her lips*) Oh no. All very hush hush. Official Secrets Act. Thirty-Year Rule. The bastard's untouchable, especially by me. It's a closed shop.

Tobias Wow.

Leila I've got proof, of course. Everything's in my briefcase: I just cleared my desk and threw everything in it. Receipts, letters, photographs, printouts of emails, videos ——

Tobias Videos?

Leila Oh yes. But I can't do a damn thing with them. I'm bound by the Act: they'd gag me and then throw me in jail for good measure if I broke it. It's the secrecy I can't abide, you know. I work so bloody hard and I can't tell anybody what I do. Nobody. Not my parents, not my friends, not anyone. They all think I'm a secretary, which in their language is a loser because I've got a bloody degree. And I see what I do out there on the streets, affecting people every day, I mean really making a difference — good or bad — and I can't say anything about it! Not in a major way, but still, it's important! (*She is pleading, trying to persuade herself*) So I'm taking all this stuff to my lawyer to deposit it and see if I can wriggle out of this.

Tobias Good idea. Sounds like your boss deserves a good kicking.

Leila See, I knew you'd come round to my way of thinking.

Tobias smiles despite himself

Casey enters from R

Casey Back to your thesis, mate. I'll take care of our clientele.

Leila It's very sweet of you to call me clientele, but my name's Leila.

Casey Hi Leila. I'm Casey. Did Tobias introduce himself?

Leila No, but I was implying that he was a bastard at the time. He may have been intimidated.

Casey Don't worry, it usually takes more than that.
Leila Oh, I have more.

Tobias goes back to the kitchen swiftly and subtly

Casey Sounds like this bloke really screwed you around.
Leila Up, around and upside-down. Let's not talk about it, eh? Tell
   me about your plan.
Casey My plan?
Leila Your dream.
Casey Oh, that. Well, I've always had an idea to open a T-shirt
   company, you know, make my own designs and slogans, maybe
   start my own label, sell them in boutiques … that kind of thing.
   I've got the designs but no money, so I'm trying to save enough
   to start up my own business.
Leila How's it going?
Casey This place? I'm just about managing to save up enough to
   pay my rent every month. It's lousy. But things might get better
   when Tobias finishes his doctorate.
Leila That's his dream, is it?
Casey Pretty much. And getting a nice cushy teaching job some-
   where. And an endless bag of tortilla chips, of course.
Tobias (*coming through to the bar*) I heard that! (*He snatches up
   the empty bowl of chips and salsa, stalks back to the kitchen and
   sits down*)
Leila Oops.
Casey Didn't deny it though, did he?
Leila You're a nice couple. I won't insult you by saying that at least
   you have each other.
Casey It's better than ——
Leila Nothing, yes. I know.

Pause

Listen, I, uh, I think I've probably had as much as I should of your
fine cocktail and I'm going to go home now before I shoot my

mouth off about any other official secrets. But I'll probably never see you kids again, so keep it to yourselves, would you? I made it all up anyhow. Delusional, you know. How much do I owe you?
Casey (*gathering Leila's card from behind the bar*) Uh, ten pounds for the jug plus three-fifty for the tortillas — thirteen-fifty.
Leila Make it fifteen. I've got the cash, actually. Here you go.
Casey (*taking the money and handing back Leila's card*) Thanks.
Leila 'S OK. It was nice to talk to you. Both of you. Thanks.
Casey Bye.
Leila Goodbye.

Leila stumbles slightly as she exits

Casey watches her go out, looks at the rest of the cocktail in the jug, grabs a couple of glasses and then calls to Tobias in the kitchen

Casey Fancy some Long Island?

Tobias gets up and comes to the doorway

Tobias Is our customer standing us a drink?
Casey In a manner of speaking. She just went off, I think the cocktail got to her.
Tobias The way you make them, I'm not surprised.
Casey Listen, the point of the bloody things is that they're strong. If she'd wanted a low-alcohol option she would have ordered Miller Lite.

Tobias makes a face. Casey pours herself a glass

Do you want some or not?
Tobias Yeah, why not? I think it might actually help with getting through the rest of Ludwig.
Casey Cheers.

Tobias comes round to the front of the bar

Tobias Cheers.

They drink

(*Noticing Leila's flashy briefcase still under the stool*) Oh *shit*.
Casey What? It's not that strong, is it?
Tobias She's left her briefcase here.
Casey Well, run out after her.

Tobias rushes out

Tobias (*off, shouting*) Leila!

Tobias returns, shrugging, without her

Couldn't see her. She must've gone into the tube.
Casey Well, we'll just keep it for her. Maybe she'll remember and
come back.

Pause

Why are you looking so worried?
Tobias Well, what if she doesn't?
Casey Come back? I suppose we open it, look for an address and
send it back, or keep it in the lost property box forever. It looks
pretty sturdy: maybe Helen can keep her guns in it.

Pause

God, cheer up! It isn't a bomb, you know!

*Tobias wanders around the case, observing and admiring it as one
might a sculpture. He leans forward and picks it up, hefting it in his
hand, feeling its weight. He strokes its surface*

Casey Tobias, why are you fondling her briefcase?
Tobias Don't you know what's in here?

Casey Papers?

Tobias Didn't she tell you?

Casey What?

Tobias Blackmail, baby, blackmail.

Casey The case is full of blackmail?

Tobias Photos, letters, disks ... videos. She was taking it to her lawyer. She wants to drop her ex in it but can't because she's gagged by the Official Secrets Act.

Casey (*not getting what he's driving at*) Well, you know, my heart bleeds. Come on Tobes, let's just stick it in the back and get this place tidy for Helen.

Tobias But *we* could, couldn't we?

Casey Are you suggesting we break into it?

Tobias No, I'm suggesting we *investigate*.

Casey Come on, Tobias, it's private! You saw the state of her. And I don't want to blackmail anyone — there's only so much trouble I'm prepared to land myself in. Look, put it down, you're making me nervous.

Tobias Bet I can guess the combination. (*He begins to fiddle with the combo lock on the front, trying different numbers*)

Casey Tobes, no, what if she comes back? What if Helen comes in?

Tobias I'll only take a second, honest — we'll just have a really quick look. (*The case pops open*) Halloooo ...

Casey What was the code?

Tobias (*smiling smugly*) 007.

Casey Oh dear, not very original. She must have been a bit of a rubbish spy. No wonder her boss gave her the elbow.

Tobias You've got to wonder, haven't you? (*He lifts the lid and begins to shuffle through the documents inside*)

Casey And what's your thesis on again?

Tobias Moral philosophy. (*He looks up innocently*) Why?

Casey You're *such* a worry. (*She comes round to the front of the bar and stares at the contents of the case*) Give us a look.

Tobias passes her a couple of photos and videos. She examines them

My God ... that's pretty — impressive.

Tobias Wish we had a video in here. Give them back.

Casey (*handing them back, looking peeved*) Why?

Tobias Like I said, we're only going to have a look. We can decide what to do with it all later. I just wanted to know what we were dealing with.

Casey What do you mean, decide what to do? She'll come back for them, of course she will. Photos like those, I would.

Tobias Casey, she drank about half a pint of vodka in that cocktail. She's probably halfway to Hammersmith by now and I'd be very surprised if she can remember she was even here, let alone how to get back. And if she's not going to claim it, don't you think we have a moral duty to carry out her wishes?

Casey What wishes?

Tobias Screwing her ex over, of course. Exposing him.

Casey Tobias, we can't blackmail this guy! He could be really important!

Tobias Those are the ones who pay the most.

Casey You know what I mean! Top-secret important. Having us killed important.

Tobias Oh please. She would have been too scared to shoot her mouth off if that had been the case. She'd be on a witness protection programme or something!

Casey Tobes, she asked me not to say anything when she left. And I think that was probably meant to include exposing her affair to the world. She wasn't just drunk, I think she was scared, probably because she'd told us too much. She'd probably already had a few before she came in. For all we know she's just tossed herself off Westminster Bridge.

Tobias (*slightly uncomfortable*) Don't be ridiculous.

Casey She asked me and I promised.

Tobias This is our big break, Casey.

Casey What?

Tobias What do you need? Money to start the business. What do I need? Money to pay off my debts. What can we get for this stuff from any newspaper in the country, the sleazier the better?

Casey We can't!

Tobias What can we get?
Casey Money! But that's not the point ——
Tobias What do we need?
Casey Stop it! (*Defeated*) Money.

Pause

You know, I really hope you never get a job teaching impression-
able young people.
Tobias Listen, after this I may not need to. I could write my book,
you could buy your shop. This is what she wanted to do with it,
Casey. She told me so. She'd love to embarrass the bastard.
Casey She told you so?
Tobias Yes.
Casey She said she'd make it public if she could?
Tobias *Yes*.
Casey (*despairing*) Oh God …

Leila enters L. *She silently takes in the scene: her case open, the
photos and papers everywhere. It seems to sober her up*

Leila Is there a problem?
Tobias *Shit*.
Casey I told you she'd come back for them.
Leila Looks like you were right. (*She walks towards them slowly*)
Well, what are we going to do?
Tobias I think we should probably give this back to you and forget
the whole thing. And apologize.

Leila cocks her head to one side, appearing to consider this

Leila That's an option, certainly. But there are others, of course.
(*She reaches her right hand slowly inside her jacket: it looks as
though she's reaching for a gun*)
Tobias Christ! Get down!

*He leaps in front of Casey and wrestles her to the ground covering
her with his body. Leila pulls a mobile phone out of her pocket and
raises an eyebrow at the cowering couple*

Leila (*answering the phone*) Hallo? … Yes. … No. … I'm just in some bar near Westminster. … Mm-hm. … No, it's under control. I'm fine. … Yeah, thanks. … Take care. (*She disconnects and returns the phone to her pocket*) What would you say if I put a proposition to you?

Casey (*instantly*) Yes.

Leila (*amused*) You haven't heard it yet.

Tobias That's OK.

Leila Well, since you're both so agreeable …

She sits down on a bar-stool. The other two slowly rise to their feet and retreat behind the bar

I want you to sell it.

Tobias Really?

Leila Yes, really. I remember I told you I wanted it out in the open, I just couldn't figure out how. You two can be my how, if you want to.

Casey How?

Leila I'm going to tell you a story, and you're going to tell this story to the papers. Are you sitting comfortably? I came in, already pissed. I sat in the corner morosely drowning my unspecified sorrows. We didn't talk except for me to order more of your industrial strength cocktails. With me so far?

Tobias Sure.

Leila I walk off sadly into the rain, leaving — oh no! — my briefcase behind. You decide to keep it for me, but the next day, when I don't come back, you open the case to try and find an address or something you can send it to me at. And you find a nice little scandal, so being honest, open citizens and believing the public has a right to know, you sell it to the highest bidder.

Casey And what's in it for you?

Leila Revenge. And half the money, obviously. Sound fair?

Tobias God, yes. I mean … thanks.

Leila It's no trouble, honestly. I was intending to take a holiday anyway. I'll let you know where to send it.

Casey But won't they investigate? Bug the place?

Leila Come on, I used to work with them. Don't you think I know all the little tricks they get up to? Well, it's getting late: I've got a plane to catch. Only other thing I need from you is collateral.

Casey Collateral?

Leila Yes, something you value. A hostage. Your credit cards, mortgage papers, whatever. Something that means I can expose you if you don't send me my cut. Got to know I can trust you, haven't I?

Casey I don't think we've got anything.

Leila Oh dear. Really?

Tobias Well, I suppose there's my — if you'd take it, I mean …

Leila What?

Tobias My thesis.

Casey Tobias, no!

Tobias It's four years' work.

Leila High stakes, eh?

Tobias For me, yes.

Leila Got it here?

Tobias goes into the kitchen, where he extracts a thick envelope, disk and a laptop case from a cupboard, looks at them for a moment, then carries them through to the bar and hands the envelope over to Leila, who weighs it in her hand

Mmm. From the weight alone I'd say it's seminal.

Tobias It needs one more chapter. On Wittgenstein. I've got two weeks to hand the whole thing in.

Leila Better get your skates on, then, hadn't you? What's the title?

Tobias "Appropriation and Opprobrium in Moral Philosophy."

Leila (*smiling*) Moral philosophy, eh? I'll look forward to reading it. Can I have the electronic copies too?

Tobias reluctantly passes her the case and a disk

Tobias Everything's on this and the laptop. Don't worry, we can't afford another computer at home.

Casey And the back-up.

He digs another disk out of his pocket and give that to Leila as well, glaring at Casey. She shrugs

It's only fair.
Leila That's very open of you, Casey; thanks. Thanks, Tobias. I think that's all I need. (*She moves to the door, stops and turns*) Well, best of luck. You seem like good kids. You know, I'm glad I found you two. I mean, it took you a while to catch on — I almost gave up when I heard you objecting, Casey — but you got there in the end. (*She winks at them*)

Casey and Tobias look at each other, perplexed

You know, it's amazing how hard it is these days to find someone who *can't* keep a secret.

Leila exits

Tobias and Casey look after her in confusion and dawning realization as the Lights fade to ——

— BLACK-OUT

FURNITURE AND PROPERTY LIST

On stage: BAR

Bar counter. *On it*: bowl of olives, cocktail sticks in container, ashtray with book matches. *Above it*: blackboard with day's specials written on it. *Behind it*: various bottles including 5 of white spirits and Coke, glasses, jug, lemon juice. *Under it*: plastic bag containing 2 T-shirts with slogans, newspapers

2 bar stools

Dishcloth

KITCHEN

Fridge

Worktops. *On them*: Microwave oven, packets of microwavable frozen ready meals, bag of tortillas, jar of cheese sauce or salsa, plates, bowls, etc., menu pad and pen

Cupboard. *In it*: white envelope containing thesis, desktop computer case, disk

Towel

Kitchen chair

Cloth for **Casey**

Library copy of Wittgenstein for **Tobias**

Off stage: Secure briefcase containing papers, photographs, videos (**Leila**)

Handbag containing a purse with debit/credit card (**Leila**)

Personal: **Casey**: wristwatch

Tobias: wristwatch, computer disk, tin of tobacco and cigarette papers in pocket

Leila: mobile phone in pocket

LIGHTING PLOT

Property fittings required: nil

Interior. The same scene throughout

To open: General interior lighting

No cues

EFFECTS PLOT

Cue 1   To open   (Page 1)
"Hits of the 80s" compilation plays in background throughout

Cue 2   **Tobias**: "God, I'm not *that* bored."   (Page 6)
Door opening and closing

www.ingramcontent.com/pod-product-compliance
Ingram Content Group UK Ltd.
Pitfield, Milton Keynes, MK11 3LW, UK
UKHW021819150726
7214IPUK00017B/217